W9-AEA-542

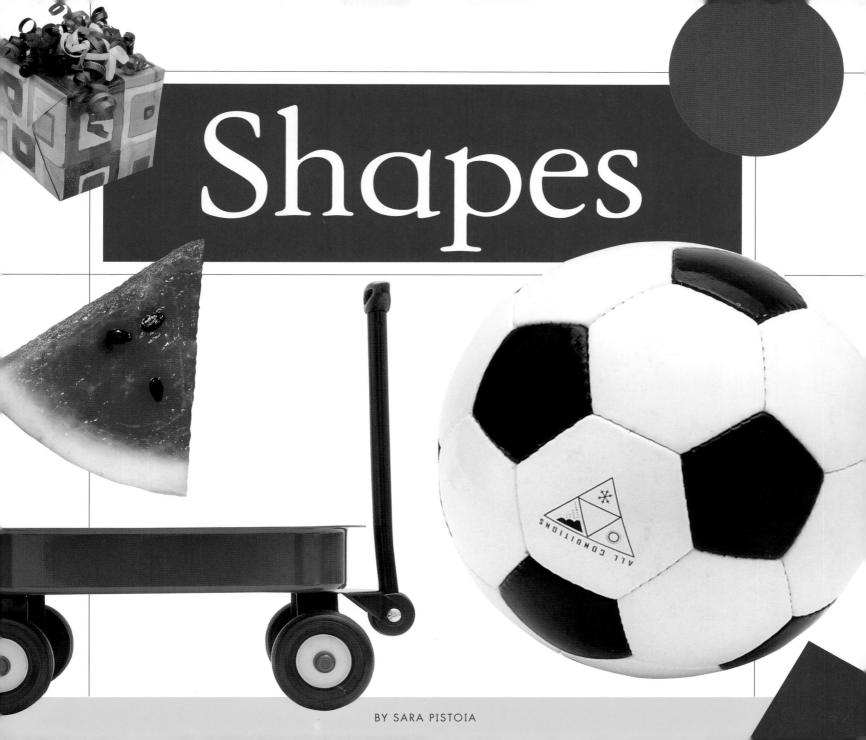

Shapes

BY SARA PISTOIA

The Child's World

Published by The Child's World®
1980 Lookout Drive • Mankato, MN 56003-1705
800-599-READ • www.childsworld.com

Acknowledgments
The Child's World®: Mary Berendes, Publishing Director
The Design Lab: Design
Editing: Jody Jensen Shaffer

Photographs ©: BrandXPictures: cover, 1, 5, 13, 22, 24; Photodisc: 4, 22, 23;
all other photographs David M. Budd Photography.

ISBN 9781623235345
LCCN 2013931775

Printed in the United States of America
Mankato, MN
July, 2013
PA02173

ABOUT THE AUTHOR

Sara Pistoia is a retired elementary teacher living in Southern California with her husband and a variety of pets. In authoring this series, she draws on the experience of many years of teaching first and second graders.

Shapes

Almost everything in our world is made of shapes.

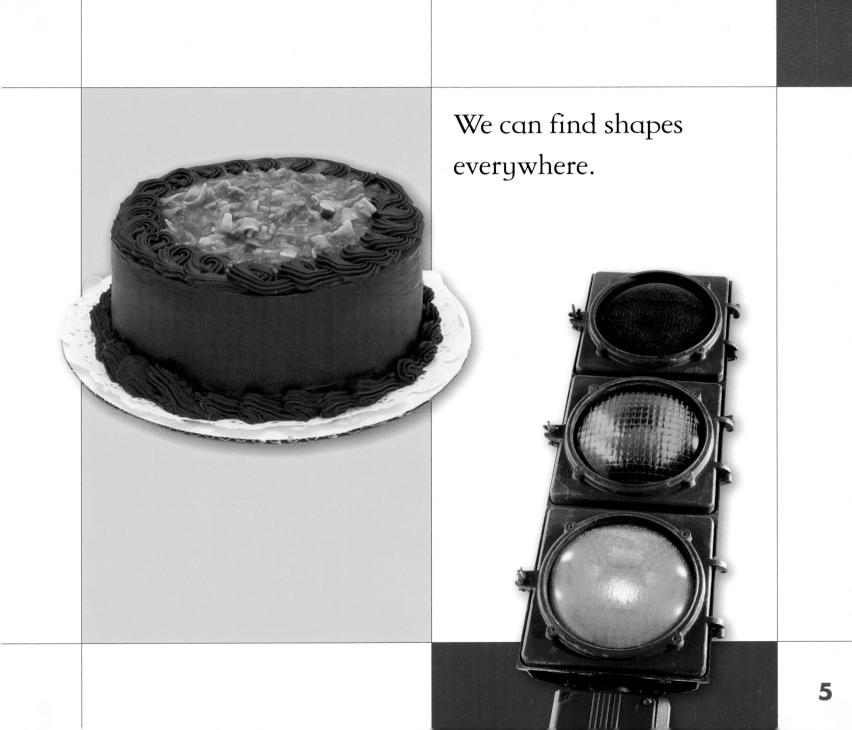

We can find shapes everywhere.

Can you name these shapes? These shapes are flat. They have two **surfaces**, a front and a back—just like a piece of paper. Flat shapes are called **plane shapes**.

If you drew a picture of this wagon, you would use plane shapes.

What shapes would help you draw the wagon?

You could draw the wagon with **circles** and a **rectangle**.

A **square** has four straight sides that are the same length.

A circle is a closed, curved line.

A **triangle** has three sides.

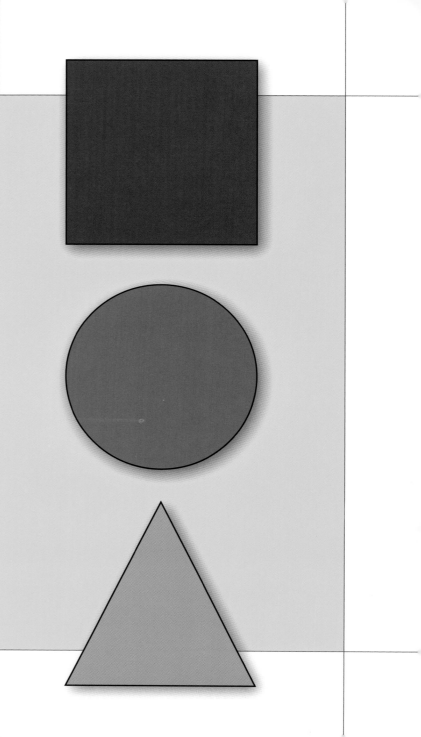

Can you draw this quilt square?

What shapes would you use?

Rectangles have four sides, but they are different from squares. They are different because two of the sides are longer.

How many squares do you see on this house?

How many rectangles do you see?

Do you ever cut a sandwich in half, from corner to corner? What shape does that make?

You end up with two triangles to eat!

Which of these triangles would you like to eat?

Some shapes are not flat like plane shapes.
Instead, they are thicker.

Usually they have more than two surfaces, too.

What are such thick shapes called?
They are **solid shapes**.

Plane shapes have two surfaces. Solid shapes usually have more surfaces.

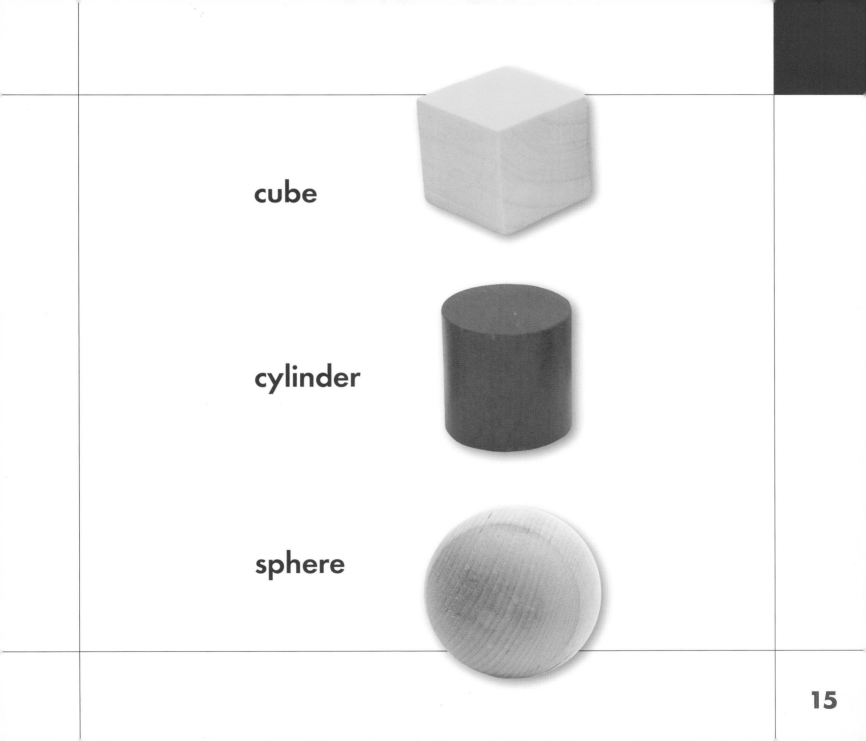

cube

cylinder

sphere

This birthday present has more than two surfaces. Its sides are square. We call this solid shape a cube.

A cube has six surfaces. This piece of birthday cake is a cube, too!

A cube is a solid shape that looks like a square. A square is flat. It has two surfaces. A cube is not flat. It has six surfaces.

A cylinder is another solid shape. It has a big curved surface. It also has a flat surface on each end.

What things are shaped like a cylinder?

You can find cylinder shapes right in your kitchen cupboard.

Jars and cans are both cylinders!

A sphere is a solid shape, too. It has only one surface. The surface is smooth and curved all over.

You probably see spheres every day. Have you played games with any of these spheres?

Plane shapes and solid shapes are everywhere.

No matter what kind they are, shapes are lots of fun!

Key Words

circles
cube
cylinder
plane shapes
rectangle
solid shapes
sphere
square
surfaces
triangle

Index